SC
ON

MARISA DONNELLY

THOUGHT CATALOG Books

BROOKLYN, NY

Thought Catalog Books is a publishing house owned by The Thought & Expression Company, an independent media group based in Brooklyn, NY. Founded in 2010, we are committed to facilitating thought and expression. We exist to help people become better communicators and listeners in order to engender a more exciting, attentive, and imaginative world. General information and submissions: manuscripts@thoughtcatalog.com. Visit us on the web at www.thought.is or www.thoughtcatalog.com.

ISBN 978-1-945796-31-9

Printed and bound in the United States.

10 9 8 7 6 5 4 3 2 1

thought.is

SOMEWHERE ON A HIGHWAY

MARISA DONNELLY

THOUGHT
CATALOG
Books

BROOKLYN, NY

Maybe you leave
because you long to know.
Maybe you leave
not because of longing
but because you must.
Or maybe you leave
simply to find the answers
you've held inside of you
all along.

SEARCHING

In the parking lot on 95th Street
I watched the sunrise
too young
to be out so late
in a dress
with a boy
who would never understand
the wild beating of my heart.
I watched the stoplights fade
red to green,
the sun gather strength
peeking between tired clouds.
I wanted to sit silent in stillness,
feel the morning air
sharp and cold
on my skin.
I wanted that boy to kiss
the bitter taste of vodka from my lips.
I wanted to get in the car of a stranger
and learn her story.
I wanted to lay in a field of grass
and let the sky swallow me whole.
I wanted anywhere but here.
I wanted more.
I wanted more.

LOVE ME UNTIL I BURN

Who would have known
just one taste
could set my heart
on fire?

4:18AM

In words we begin our escape—
notes on the edges of papers
scrawled sentences in journals
unspoken secrets running wild in our heads,
only revealing themselves when we close our eyes.

We whisper our wishes at night, our bodies
curled tightly, knees to our chests like children.
Only when the sun goes down
do we allow ourselves to dream
to imagine our hips swaying in the moonlight
of another city, another town, hands held by a stranger
who will soon steal a piece of our soul under that dark sky.

The escape always begins with words—
confessing our longings
to search
until we find what we're missing
until we find what we've lost
until we find we are not the only one
awake at night with a pounding heart.

SIXTEEN

I was always running
away
from the sound of my mother's voice
his hand around my waist
the streets whispering my name
saying I must stay,
seek shelter
where my feet felt familiar.
But I'd learned young
the ways of catch and release.
A softball pitcher, I knew a tight hold
on the ball only made the leather slip
from my grasp.
Sometimes strength
was discovered
in letting go,
watching that ball
loosen, lift
then soar.
So I took off
like I always did
running
into the silence of night,
shoes on asphalt
the only sound.

YOU WERE EVERYTHING I SHOULDN'T, AND EVERYTHING I SHOULD

I should have known
your kiss
would taste like rebellion.

I should have known
those lips
would hurt and heal.

ALMOST LOVE

I held his hand
as if I hadn't felt the palm
hundreds of times before,
all of my words
interlaced
in our quiet fingertips.
I kissed those lips—
they tasted like mint and rum
stolen from his parents' kitchen cabinet.

I kissed and kissed
until I could almost forget
how restless I'd become.

MAYBE THIS IS WHY

Maybe our bodies
are just hearts
with legs
and that's why we're so quick
to run.

THIS WILD HEART

I wasn't supposed to feel
anxious
eager
one foot out the door
and eyes straight ahead
forgetting
to look back.

I wasn't supposed to feel
so ready
at eighteen
my heart filled by worlds
I hadn't yet experienced.

I wasn't supposed to feel
so pulled
to leave this town
this boy
this mother's touch
meant to keep me safe.

But I was always one
to drive well over the speed limit
whiskey still wet on my lips.
I was always one to jump
too quickly, too fully.

Even then, age eighteen,
I knew I wasn't meant
to be safe.

THE SUMMER BEFORE I LEFT
FOR COLLEGE

I was dizzy in love
with the idea of love
so much so
I expected boys
who were not men
to chase me

when what I really wanted
was to chase
everything that didn't taste
like home.

IOWA STARS

Look at the stars, I said to my mother,
my forehead pressed against the passenger-side window
neck craning to get a glimpse of that Midwest sky.
Please look at them.
Thousands, sparkling white and bright
against the black backdrop around us
so beautiful they didn't seem real.
I-35 was silent, not a car in sight,
the moon shining over us
bold and brilliant.
It was mile 401, almost to my destination,
a small town where no one knew my name.
My mother reached for my hand and squeezed my fingers,
a simple gesture not always exchanged
between a stubborn Pisces
and her strong-minded Leo mother.
We didn't speak for a moment,
the sky taking all our breath away.

As the miles rolled on, we talked about boys
about laughter, about growing up and the passage of time.
Her voice was soothing, like the lullabies
sung to me when I was a child,
soft and familiar.
The highway slipped past our quiet tires,
streetlights specks in the distance.
I lost all sense of time,
out of place from my suburban town,
seeking solace in our silence.
As we drove on, I watched the stars
their quiet elegance
magical, twinkling, unafraid.
And on that unfamiliar highway
I didn't feel so lost.

IMPERMANENCE

You and I
were never meant to last
too many elbows, too much skin
two bodies intertwined
in beds
but never dreams.
And when I close my eyes
on silent Saturday nights,
willing my body to sleep
to the steady sound of your breathing
I can't help but imagine myself
a thousand places
a thousand cities
a thousand miles
away
from your arms.

MIDWRESTLESS

I drive these Illinois highways
these long Iowa backroads
blacktop blending to gravel
as the sun sets.

I keep the music loud
the windows down
one arm stretched out
to feel the breeze on my fingertips.

95 on the highway
I feel weightless
the pavement opening
to me, pulling me farther
and farther from the familiar.

I watch the wheat fields
fade in my rearview,
blurs of blue and green
earth and tired sky.

Tonight I'll drive until I run out of gas
chasing the sun.

RUN WILD WITH ME

Take off your shoes, and let's go. Let's run
barefoot through this little town, let's race
along the edge of the highway,
our soles marking paths behind us.

I don't want my life to fit in a little box, to bend,
to mold, to be a certain shape. I want to lean my head back
and take in the sky and all its colors.
I want to stick out my tongue and lick the fresh rain.
I want to squish my toes into dirt and lay
in the green grass and close my eyes.

I don't want to follow rules,
but make my own, soaking
up this earth and all the sunshine.

So please, run wild with me.

Take off in the car with no destination,
wind whipping through the open windows
drowning all sound.

Let's make animals of the clouds. Let's count the stars
when the sky darkens. Let's keep driving until we run
out of gas and make an adventure of wherever we land.

I'm no good at toeing a line, at always following
the footsteps of those before me.

My father was a thinker, my mother an artist
and so I've always dreamed
too big for my own good.

Run wild with me.
Taste the flavors of the earth on your tongue,
drink in the sky, the sounds, the smells.
I cannot be rooted
to four walls, to one town.

I'm like the sun, forever chasing the moon.
I rise anew at every dawn.

My feet are tired, my soles worn.
But I won't ever stop running,

So come with me.

AND IT BEGAN

She felt the interstate shift under her feet
each step, a promise
of who she would one day become.

WANDERING

DIRECTIONLESS

She lost herself on the edge of 10th Street
where the pavement dead-ended into gravel
and the trees stretched for miles

maybe the sun called out to her
shining fearlessly through the clouds

maybe her breath caught in her chest
like the moment before she cries

or maybe that sinking feeling
of not knowing where she was anymore
or if the world would be the same when she turned around

and so she kept moving forward
dust billowing around her feet,
an unconscious goodbye.

WANDERLUST

I am a knapsack
tied to an abandoned birch branch.
I am a pebble along the shoulder
of a four-lane highway, Route 55
westbound
chasing the sun.
I am a heads-up penny
on the floor of a nonstop train
Chicago to Seattle.
I am the white, feathery seed
of a dandelion
flirting with the wind.
I am the worn soles
of a pair of Converse
speckled with rainwater and mud.

And you are time.

We move together
passionate
lovers.

Each other's desire,
each other's demise.

AND THAT MOMENT BECAME POETRY

Let's chase the stars, were the most romantic words
he ever whispered to me, his body so terrifyingly beautiful
next to mine in the back of his truck like a goddamn cliché.

I was always good at being poetic,
at making a sliver of memory blossom in my mind.
But the way we were angled, the bed of that truck tilted
off the mountainside, overlooking Phoenix
and all her blinking lights—I got caught up
in the rush, the flurry of motion, miles and miles below.

And us, silent on the mountain.

We were wrapped in his childhood blanket. He kissed
me on my forehead, slid his hands along the hem of my dress.
He held my head tenderly, as if I were fragile, and I let him.

He kissed me and I stared up at the sky,
drinking in the midnight black.
The night seemed endless. I wanted to hold
the stars in the palm of my hand.
I wanted to drink the moment in and commit it to poetry.

I didn't want to ever forget.

He kissed me, and I thought of all the names
of the constellations,
all the patterns I had yet to trace, all the world
I had yet to feel underneath my feet.

I watched the city blink at us, blink at the stars, one cycle
of light and color and movement,
and I felt small.

He kissed me again and I was dizzy,
Arizona heat making my head heavy.

I wanted to explain this to him—the heat, the stars,
our simple existence.
I wanted to have him look into my eyes,
to watch them sparkle like the patterns above us,
blinking, reflecting their own brown light.

I imagined our minds, our bodies, our hands intertwined,
sitting in silence, taking in the mystery.

But I couldn't find the words.
Not words he would understand.

So I took deep breaths. In, then out.
My every exhale evaporating
into those constellations,
that sky, tiny
and insignificant.

3:30AM

The roads called at night, always
long and lonesome and winding.

She always drove
with one hand on the wheel,
the windows rolled down,
the gas pressed just a little too far.

This was her way of running
when her legs couldn't carry her
fast enough.

HE SAID HE LOVED ME

And I believed him
because words, for me, carried weight
because I felt safe
because I liked how forever looked
in his arms.
He was the first
to let those words
roll off his tongue,
a promise
he never intended to keep.
I tried to kiss
away the emptiness
screaming, "I love you"
into the spaces
as if I could fill
him,
us.
He was my first
experience with transience—
searching for a residence
in the impermanent.

FINDING MY WAY BACK

I can close my eyes and still remember
the way the earth smelled like gravel and sunburnt skin,
the cheap gas-station vodka burning my throat,
a boy's hand on the small of my back,
the black, black sky watching my every move.

Whenever I was dizzy and drunk
on freedom and loneliness
I would look up
to right myself again.

And the sky, those roads, these stars
would guide my tired heart home.

FOR HIM

I want you to know I wrote about you today.

Writing you was easy. Writing you was hard.
With every word I felt a catch in my throat
I couldn't explain.
Some strange way of falling
for you, even still.

I wrote you a poem.
Long and liquid
words like wounds
reopening, spilling blood
across the surface of each page.

I wrote every secret, every hope,
every wish
confessing how my lips
still long
to be kissed
by yours.

I wrote my thoughts,
my stories, my heart.
All for you,
the sweet soul
I once loved,

and you'll never read them.

I keep telling myself,
better without your eyes.

LOST & FOUND

I was twelve when I ran away from home.
Barefoot. T-shirt. December. 9:31PM.

I remember my feet on the icy pavement
as if they weren't a part of my body.

Numb
Weightless

I wasn't cold. The breath entered my lungs
sharp, fierce, a reminder I was here,
I was alive.

Every girl almost a woman falls into a moment
where she wants to stop
breathing
where she wants to scream and shatter glass
break the barrier she built around her mother's heart
around her own heart, cold and afraid.

I was twelve, running without a map

without a destination
listening to the way
my breathing mixed into the silence
of a winter night.

I was feeling everything
I was feeling nothing.

Standing in the snow,
I couldn't be more lost.
An unknown street
An unknown hour
No home to call.

But in all the white,
the steady rhythm of heartbeat
and bare soles on pavement,
I am found.

IF YOU ARE THE WIND

If you are the wind,
I am stretching
myself across you
with your weightless
arms open like sails.

If you are the wind,
I am whispers, lost,
coalescing, transforming into one
quiet rush.
Silence.

If you are the wind,
I am a soaring bird
wings beating, heart
pumping, matching stroke
for gust.

If you are the wind,
I am a dandelion seed, twisting,
spinning, caught
in your embrace,
traveling miles, seeing a sky
I'd never dreamed
until now.

But you are not the wind.
And I am standing on the edge
of a hill, watching the snowflakes
swirl around me,
my face pink
and cold.

EIGHTEEN

Late at night, when I couldn't sleep, I pulled
myself from the covers of my dormitory bed,
walked barefoot
on the cool asphalt and lay
in the middle of the deserted, small-town street,
permitting the September air to soak
my skin and the lightning bugs to flit around my hair.

I stayed in the street and stared into the expanse of sky.

A sky that promised new beginnings
with every flickering star.

THIS ONE'S FOR YOU

Do you remember
the little black car,
driving miles from Fresno to Pismo,
my bare feet out the passenger window,
nails painted pink?
The days were sunny, hot.
The nights were always hot.
Do you remember
sushi, flower-shaped and salmon,
you across the table making eyes at me,
my hand on your thigh, laughing.
Always laughing.
Do you remember
waking in tangled bed sheets,
California to Chicago,
across the Midwest,
cold fingertips, naked skin?

We knew life wouldn't stay easy.

For us, we unfolded no roadmaps,
no tire treads to follow
from West Coast dirt
to Midwest snow.

If I could give you my heart like an atlas,
I'd let your fingers trace the highways,
the veins that make the backroads,
the creeks, pauses where you've taken my breath.

But until then, I'll close my eyes,
wish away the Midwest winter,
and feel summer wind on my face,
bare toes extended out open windows,
reaching for the sun.

FINDING CLARITY

A stretch of highway in Colorado
dips behind the clouds and does not
distinguish between asphalt and sky.
I turn off the music, turn off the lights,
drive slowly in silence
the stars
my only guide.

WE'RE BECOMING LOVE

You take my hand in yours with tenderness
like my fingers are the most beautiful you've ever held
and suddenly it makes sense.
I've been smiling at temporary faces
looking into temporary eyes
kissing temporary lips
touching temporary bodies
searching
for you.

I ALWAYS LOVE WHAT NEVER LASTS

I'm in love with the fleeting—
smiles that pass quickly between strangers,
toenail polish that never stays.

Sometimes I wonder if beginnings have endings
or if endings are only beginnings of something else.

I love the first breath of morning, slipping
in and out of sleep.
I love when eyes open, slowly, still hesitant and afraid.

What doesn't last is the most powerful—
skipping heartbeats, sweaty palms.

What stays becomes comfortable, easy.

We forget the beauty of a cliff or field of wheat.
We recognize the power of a bank of clouds
only in the dull blue of a sky.

We ache for the zing of a strawberry
when we can no longer taste the seeds—
like remembering you,
bitter and beautiful on my tongue.

THIS YOU MUST LEARN YOUNG:

Go.
Run.
Leave.
Never stop.
For you were not born
to stay still.

YOU ALMOST HAD ME

You will always remind me
of late nights on I-35,
Three Musketeers bars melting
chocolate all over my fingers
and you laughing,
leaning in to kiss the sweetness
from my lips.

I wish I could go back
and unfold my stubborn arms,
feel the scruff of your beard
underneath my palms
again,
tell you
you were
the only man
who made me
believe
even those born to run
might learn to slow down.

IN YOUR ABSENCE

Absence makes the heart grow fonder.

I knew absence
like I knew you,
the freckles on your right shoulder blade
just above the raised lines of a tattoo,
Japanese word for strength
etched over each vertebra,
ink fading blue-black into your skin.

I knew fondness
like I knew November snow
melting on my flushed cheeks,
like I knew traffic on I-88,
like I knew that sign at 4th
in front of your apartment
where no one stops.

At twenty-one,
I thought I knew
Everything,
thought I knew love
when I could feel a heart pulsing
in a body under my fingertips.

But maybe I was wrong.

I never thought
I'd be the one to turn away,

I never thought
you'd respond with absence.

And I never thought
that I would be the one, years later
still writing fond poems
about the boy I left.

HE MADE HER THE SUN

and so she became the rays, rising
bold and bright each day, filling
his world with warmth, light, energy.

The darkest parts of him,
his roots, twisted and buried
deep underground,
stretched out to her, breaking
from the dirt. And he opened
his leaves to her,
pulling her in.

She was consistent,
waking every morning
loving him through snow,
peeking around rain clouds
to kiss his face.

He made her the sun.
But now he chases
the moon,
looking for the same light
from a duller star.

And she,
she shines.

THE ONES WHO ARE LEFT BEHIND

The one who leaves always has it easy.

My mother whispers as we watch
the first boy I ever loved walk
to his car from my bedroom window,
my heart aching with the weight
of breaking
his.

Tomorrow morning, the sun will bring
me new beginnings, a new life, new school six hours away.
Tomorrow morning, the sun will bring
me miles on a highway
while he stares at his ceiling
searching
for answers.

The one who leaves,
leaves with a fuller heart.

Roads become blurred in the rearview
while the one who's left behind
must learn how to breathe,
connect the pieces,
wipe away the tread of the tires
imprinted
in the cracks on his ceiling.

HIGHWAY 9

I wonder if you know
I still think about you
every time I drive
the gravel backroad
where we first kissed,
electricity between us sparking white
against that night sky like fireflies.

I wonder if you feel the rush too,
years later on another road
in another town—
the bitter taste
of loss on your lips.

FRAGMENTS

You have a piece of my soul
in some corner of the world
in some city where you rest your head
not thinking, in the slightest,
about me.
Our connection
is paper thin—or, like sutures,
weaving through the sinews of my heart,
stitching fragments of you to me, of me to you
to your chest cavity, laying claim,
filling those hollow spaces,
making you whole
so you won't miss me,
haven't missed me
since I've been gone.

I hate knowing I am a piece of you,
some small speck of matter across your lips,
some miniature brain cell buried
behind new memories
new faces,
new bodies.

I hate knowing webs knot between us,
keeping us together, keeping us trapped,
suffocated,
by what we believed was love.

Maybe walking away
will tear our surgical silk,
will render our spider's thread.

Maybe we'll always be connected
across the expanse of space and sky,
and when I lift my head from the pillow,
you'll feel my energy too. You'll wonder
why you've felt so restless
ever since I left.

ON AN IOWA BACKROAD

What if we just did it? I asked,
Did what we were thinking?
Said what we wanted?
Kissed without wondering
whether or not we should?

He was driving too fast
and I was drunk,
the Iowa cornfields blurring
outside my window,
gravel dust spinning around the car.

He looked at me,
didn't say anything
always matching my words
with his silence,
saying more
than I ever could.

I wonder if he knew I was dizzy,
I was foolish,
I was already contemplating
how I could lean across that center console
and put my mouth on his.

I wonder if he knew I was dizzy,
I was foolish,
that minutes later
at the stop sign
I would.

I wonder if he knew I was dizzy,
I was foolish,
and almost got lost in that kiss
in those lips.

I wonder if he knew I was dizzy,
I was foolish,
and had already started
breaking his heart.

AUGUST, 2011

I can't stop running
from all the people
I shouldn't be running from.

THIS WANDERING HEART

You leave
because you have to,
because leaving is necessary,
because your survival
depends on letting your soul shift
in the wind like a grain of sand.

You leave
because your heart will ache
if you stay
even if your bones will ache
when you go.

You leave
because you don't love him.
You leave
because you do.

You leave
because of fear
and in spite of it.

You leave
because you are strangely at home
in a place not yet familiar.

You leave
because a force,
a pull,
a tug on your soul
you have yet to understand.

You leave
for reasons you can't explain
and for reasons you won't.

You leave
simply because you cannot be here.
Or maybe you leave
because you've never learned
to stay.

WE RAN OUT OF FOREVERS

He stood at my front door, a mess of brown curls
and timid hands
and those blue-green eyes that never revealed
his true intentions.
I fell into his arms, a familiar pattern
that suddenly felt strange.

You're leaving.

His voice was a breath,
a candle wavering in the wind.

I didn't say anything but held him tighter to my chest,
feeling for his heartbeat through his T-shirt.

I'm not leaving.
I'm going.

There's a difference.
There has always been a difference.

This is what I told myself.
What I tell myself still.

Leaving meant permanence.
A permanence I was not ready to admit.

I'm not leaving forever.

But by stepping out the front door
I already had.

AUGUST, 2016.

Saying goodbye
was like inhaling oxygen
like a knot wrapped around my ribs
untying, loosening,
releasing,
opening,
learning to breathe again.

NOW THAT SHE'S GONE

Why do they always slither back
like snakes on their bellies
after she leaves?

Last night I dreamt about a cobra.
I was staring the snake in the eyes,
tempting fate,
trying to calm my nerves,
to pretend I was unafraid
the way I've learned to act with all men,
my chest puffed out like a sparrow,
all utterances from my lips
loud and bold like a song.

They never know the worth of a strong woman
until she's no longer theirs,
until her wings have taken her
miles away from their arms.
They never know how to love a strong woman
until she's gone,
until they realize
all she needed
was to fly
without her wings being clipped.

YOU'LL ALWAYS BE MY FOREVER

I saw a picture of you last night
and now I can't get you out of my head.

You're still the same green-grey eyes,
the crooked smile, the hair falling
in your face like you haven't combed since I left.
Maybe no one's there to brush anymore, no one
to pull your hair back, run their fingers
through the curls, kiss
the tender baby hairs at your temple.

When I saw the picture, I heard your voice,
the way you used to know what I was thinking
by the way my eyebrows furrowed
or the unconscious bite of my lip.
The tendencies I never noticed, even in myself.

My mother always told me you looked different
in every photograph—as if she could see your transformation
before the changes even began. As if she knew
who you'd become.
That you'd run.
But she never imagined I'd be the one
to leave. That I was the one in the photographs
shifting with every frame.

I called you last night. Because I saw the picture,
because I wanted to know if your voice still sounded
like Saturday mornings with closed blinds,
an old truck with the windows down on the highway
in the sticky-hot Western sun. Yes, you did.

Your voice brought me to all the places I'd been searching for,
all the places I'd been pretending not to miss.

You're still the green-grey eyes, the laugh
that warms me. You're still the unbrushed hair.

And I promise I'll run my fingers through the tangles.
Promise I'll kiss every lonely strand,
every broken follicle.

Until you can taste the forever on my lips.

WHAT THEY DON'T TELL YOU
ABOUT LEAVING

I wasn't prepared for all my goodbyes.
The hills. The Midwest green.
The roads that held my biggest secrets.
The arms of the boy I loved
but never told how I truly felt.

I wasn't ready to turn around,
to put my key in the ignition,
to close my eyes, steady my breath,
and feel the car hum to life beneath my feet.

I wasn't ready to drive past that hill with the gas station
where I slid my car into the snowbank, tipsy,
or where I cried, head pressed to the steering wheel
for my sister, hundreds of miles away,
whom I could no longer protect.

I wasn't ready to leave the old apartment on K Street
where I'd loved and lost and gave my heart away.
I wasn't ready to drive on those gravel paths
where I'd run, night after night, letting my feet carry me
when I hardly had the strength to continue
and where tears would fall,
cleansing me, healing me
in ways that only feet on pavement can.

I wasn't ready to let go of the hands I'd held,
the lips I'd kissed, the bodies I'd pulled close to mine
in moments of celebration and loneliness, on late nights

and early mornings, on days when friends became family
and those small-town streets felt like home.

I wasn't ready to say goodbye to the school,
to the stores, to the people, to the strangers.

I wasn't ready to say goodbye to me,
to the woman I'd become, passionate,
resilient.

But somehow I turned the key, pulled on my seatbelt,
changed the radio station because I couldn't bear the silence.
Somehow I merged onto that highway, those trees fading
in the rearview
like a part of me
disappearing into dewy, morning air.

I acted like leaving was easy.
Because I was supposed to.
Because my time had finally arrived.
Because I couldn't stay.

But leaving was a kind of death.

I can travel thousands of miles from Midwest fields,
from gravel roads, from cottonwood trees
And I'll still ache for the smell of grass, for dirt
underneath my fingernails, for the taste
of a cold beer under an Iowa sunset.

No matter how far I run,
the sunset follows me.

BECOMING

YOU & ME ON I-35

Sometimes life is simple,
my feet on the dashboard
your fingers in my hair
the windows down
and our worries in the rearview.

BELONGING

A picture frame behind my childhood bed
shared facts about the date I was born.

March Sixth
A Pisces

My sign told me I was strong.
I was sensitive.
I was fluid:
made of water,
never fixed to one place.

When I was younger, I used to trace
the edge of the frame
the letters of my name printed at the top,
like a declaration
of who I'd be
of who I'd become.

Marisa
Of the sea

Perhaps I was never meant
to wander on my tired feet.

Perhaps they ache
after long days
because the soles bear the weight
of a world
where they will never
belong.

HOME WAS NEVER A PLACE, YOU KNOW

Your smile
those green eyes
the way I tasted the ocean salt
like freedom
on your lips.

You tell me California's too hot,
you miss the Midwest sting.

But I wonder if you long
for the little apartment,
frost on the windows,
and our toes touching
under the faded grey quilt.

Maybe you don't miss the cold at all,
but the sound of my voice
making anywhere we wandered
feel like home.

DANCING IN MY MOTHER'S HEELS

I remember trying on my mother's heels. Twirling,
transfixed at the reflection in the bathroom mirror.

Woman. The word lay heavy and unsure on my tongue.

I was breast buds and bare feet, overalls that didn't quite fit
and a different color polish on every fingernail. Falling,
meant off the swing set. Fear
was closing my eyes without the closet light. Men
were my father and the neighbor who carried me home
when I split my shin on concrete. Boys
were the ones who ran shirtless and raced me
on their bikes and peed in my sandbox.

I didn't yet know what my heels could do,
what a mirror could say. What a girl
gains, gives, grows.

Why the word *woman* was so terrifying.

I danced in those heels. Danced and twirled and twisted
and laughed at my flush-faced reflection. *Woman. Woman.*

Later, my mother would wipe the color from my lips.
My father would kiss me to sleep with his lullabies.

Brown-eyed girl, brown-eyed girl. Not a woman. Not yet.

Sometimes when I stand in the mirror, I trace the muscles
of my calves. The transformation, the curves of my skin.
I wonder about that girl,
twirling in a dress and shoes too big.

I used to be afraid of that face, that body, those legs.

Now I know better.

Those heels are power. Mine to take, to give.

Woman. Strong.

And I still twirl in the mirror. *Brown-eyed girl, brown-eyed girl.*

DEAR SEVENTEEN,

This is a poem to let you know
you survive—
the unsettling heartbreak
eating a hole in your chest,
your mother's anger,
the alcohol on your breath
chasing your words with sips
until your voice was unintelligible
until you didn't have to speak at all
until that bourbon burned
the back of your throat
drowning out all feeling.

You survive.

You were spiraling, spiraling,
trying to fill yourself
with liquid courage,
with some false sense
of confidence,
of love.
You were dying to leave,
dying to escape.
You were dying.
Waking from dreams,
twisted in bedsheets,
lost
and longing.

But you survive.

You let go.
You burned your pain,
held the ashes in your palm
and set them free into the sky.

You were always stronger
than you believed, Seventeen.

And listen, in two years, you will fall in love;
in three, your heart will be broken again.
In one, you will leave the home you've known
and in six, you will leave for good
and all the mystery won't ache anymore.

In six and a half years, you will fall asleep
to the sound of cars rushing by your window.
You will be warm. You will be unafraid.

In six and a half years, you will know
who you are.
And you will find she's the same woman
you've always been.

WHEN I THINK ABOUT YOU, AND TIME

I used to believe
time was running out,
and if we didn't have answers,
if you didn't say those words
I needed to hear
when I needed to hear them
we would cease
to be anything
and change would swallow us whole,
spitting us out in two different parts of the world,
and we'd forget
who we once were.
In many ways, I was right.
You left.
I ran.
You didn't come back.

And I watched the sun set
on your memory.
But now I understand
time never mattered
with love—with us.
You can't erase
a person's touch from your memory
or stop your heart from beating
at the mention of a name.
Real love
is never about the hours
the months
the years
nestling between two bodies.
With you and I,
the clock will never stand a chance.

SOMEWHERE ON A HIGHWAY

My best thinking
is done alone.
I've told all my exes,
but somehow solitude always sounds
like an excuse.
They've never understood
when I lace up those shoes,
when I get in that car,
I feel my body come alive,
strengthened by an open road,
a path that despite the tread
always feels new,
untouched.
A highway cleanses—
my feet to the gravel
or foot on the gas,
destination lost in yellow lines,
in faded street signs
and the woman I used to be
in the rearview.

In all the cities I've traveled,
I feel like I've left
a piece of myself behind
while finding
who I really was at every exit.
I like the way the silence
rushes with the wind past my face
or how I lose feeling in my fingers
when I hold them out to the open air.
I empty my mind
somewhere on a highway,
letting the thoughts drift
and fill space around me.
I feel free
somewhere on a highway
where time is endless
and I choose
where I will go
and who I will become.

DEAR YOU,

I hope you feel soft today,
I hope the world carries you
on her shoulders like a precious child
swaddled in her warm embrace.
I hope you let go
Of every fear and uncertainty
Of every dark cloud hanging
like an omen above your head.
I hope wherever she takes you
that you will learn to call the place home
And that you will let the sky fill you
with rain when you are emptied
like a bucket overflowing,
spilling off the edges,
quenching the thirst
of our broken earth
Until you no longer ache
for anything but your steady legs
and the ground beneath your feet.

I DO NOT MISS HIM ANYMORE

In my new place, I keep no memories of him.

His pictures do not cover the walls, and his body
does not lurk behind every stop sign, every street corner,
every aisle of the grocery store just waiting
to make my heart skip a beat again.

I do not think of him when I first wake up,
when I look out the window, when I glance at my
new shelf new bed new closet new apartment new life.

No, I don't imagine him just up the road,
rolling out of bed with his hair all askew
and a sleepy smile.

I don't think about the places
where we kissed or the laughter that coated
every crowded hallway, every open room.

He is nonexistent here, only alive in my memory.
And I want to keep him contained.

Far from my reach, far from my sight, far enough
that when I close my eyes late at night
I can't remember the sound of his sleepy breathing,
can't remember the feeling of his hand
on the small of my back,
can't remember how to love someone
who doesn't love you enough

because I'm 2,000 miles away

with only my heartbeat keeping me company,

and I'm the happiest I've ever been.

LETTING GO.

And suddenly you forgot. You laughed and cried.
You drank cocktails and watched the sun set
over white clouds.
You ran and biked and listened
to the sound of your own voice.
Speaking out loud. Speaking without fear.
You took pictures again.
Ones where you smiled at the camera.
Ones where you didn't look away.
You wrote poetry and drank tea at the table
in a pair of fuzzy slippers.
You drove without changing the radio station
and sang as loud as you could.

You forgot what loneliness meant.
And remembered how you felt when whole.

FOR YOU, WILD WOMAN

You were never foolish for kissing him,
for looking deep into his eyes,
for losing your footing like a teenager,
stumbling and drunk on love.
You were never wrong for wanting a sacred place,
some quiet corner of the universe
you could claim as your own.
You were young.
And you were searching, even then.
But you were trying to make homes
out of temporary people.
Trying to find yourself in the body of a stranger
who could never fill you, never complete you,
never satisfy the longing in your chest
to be both protected and set free,
both loved and let go.

You were born with wandering feet and a heart
already whole.
You weren't meant to be held, to be caged,
to be saved
You were meant to run.
Born to grab the earth with your fingertips,
taste the wild and uncharted on your tongue.

HOME.

I have found a home
in two legs and a heartbeat,
in brown eyes that hold secrets,
in lips that whisper words
carefully, testing them first
before making a sound.

I have found a home
in tired hands
in nails too long
hips and calves that bear the weight
of every promise
and every future dream.

I have found a home
in a woman
strong,
fierce,
and loved.

And she smiles back at me
in the bathroom mirror.

Proud
and unafraid.

BECOMING

A drumbeat breaks the silence
boldly declaring a presence
on the beach
where we lay in various stages
of wake and sleep,
of coming and going,
of breathing in and letting go.

I am on the sand
writing poetry,
blinking in the light
that breaks through West Coast clouds
demanding to be seen,
to be felt.

A homeless man beats the drum,
a white, ripped T-shirt, dirty hands,
golden blond curls
that blend in the sun.

His head is tilted back, eyes closed,
feeling the beat through fingertips.

I close my eyes, too, and listen to him,
to the scattered voices,
to the seagulls begging for scraps,
to the bartenders and the clinking of glasses,
to the waves breaking on the shore in succession,
each one stronger than the last.

Maybe the rhythm teaches me how
to finally know
to finally be at home
in my own skin.

Maybe I was always meant
to run until I was forced to slow,
forced to breathe deeply,
to close my eyes and soak
in the sound of a steady
drum played by hands
that see beauty in each grain of sand.

Maybe I've finally discovered
how to sit still,
to trust,
to seek.

Maybe where the sky and the water
and the sand meet
my new story begins.
I am just now
in my infinite moment
becoming.

TWENTY-THREE

And so you became. Your soul felt lighter, shifting
with the weight of change. You stopped trying to fit
and started to just *be*. Imperfect and flawed,
tough and soft
tender and strong.

You were a body with a beating heart
and a mind that ceased to wander.
You stayed up late and woke up early,
swallowing the sky whole and spitting clouds
in your poetry, more wild and vibrant than before.

You danced. You laughed. You learned.
how life is a series of give and take,
and you must grab hold of what you can.

You believed in happiness again,
letting peace flow through you, letting love grow
and bloom, bold and beautiful around your feet.

You watched the stars,
stopped trusting them to save you
and instead took in their splendor.

You were all things soft: a feather, a candle
a kiss on a tired cheek. But you were not weak.
You took the world and made all yours.

And yes, you became.

TO JUST BE

I was always *rush rush rush*
trying to run in the right direction
trying to know what and where and who I should be.

Lately, I am quiet.

Lately, I love how the sun rests effortlessly on my face,
or the way my body recognizes a good song.

Lately, I let the wind kiss my cheeks
and I soak in the sound of someone else's laughter.

Lately, I watch the dawn break through cloudy skies
and run blades of grass between my fingertips,
no place to be.

Lately, in the silence, my mind is loud.

Lately, my heart feels full
with clouds, earth, and wind.

Lately, I cry on open highways
where the road seems endless and untouched—
the cry of knowing I'm headed somewhere I'm destined to be.

See, we're all searching to be found.

Life is a beautiful Sunday morning,
and I'm the only car on the highway.

And lately, I like being lost

MARISA DONNELLY

Marisa Donnelly is a Midwest-born, West Coast-based writer, poet, and essayist whose work specializes in relationships, love, heartbreak, faith, traveling, growth and self-discovery.

She is the author of two emotional essay compilations, *Big Heart Problems* and *Fiercely Independent* (*Most Days*) and her writing appears both in print and online, at Thought Catalog, Quote Catalog, and her personal blog, Word & Sole, among others.

She currently resides in sunny San Diego, California

ABOUT THE PUBLISHER

Thought Catalog Books is a publishing house owned by The Thought & Expression Company, an independent media group based in Brooklyn, NY. Founded in 2010, we are committed to facilitating thought and expression. We exist to help people become better communicators and listeners in order to engender a more exciting, attentive, and imaginative world.

Visit us on the web at
www.thought.is or www.thoughtcatalog.com